sun memos
ziggy alberts

first edition

First published 2024.

©2024 Ziggy Alberts. All rights reserved. No part of this work may be reproduced, stored in a retrieval system, or transmitted in any form or by any means, electronic, electrostatic, magnetic tape, mechanical, photocopying, recording or otherwise without prior permission in writing of the publisher.

A catalogue record for this book is available from the National Library of Australia at catalogue.nla.gov.au

Cover and internal photos by Ziggy Alberts
Internal illustrations by Shaela Templeton
Book design and layout by Tango Media Pty Ltd

ISBN 978-0-6487057-6-5

ziggyalberts.com
commonfolkpublishing.com

PART I.

Buddhist Hotline

Scars aren't proof
that you've been hurt
scars are proof
that you have healed.
-

chicks dig scars
and so do men

The one time
taking more
and not less
is always right
and is seldom practiced
is in humans
and all the good advice
we each
so willingly
give.

Usually
our first reaction
when diving into a frigid sea
is to hold
our breath
to restrict
our breathing

isn't it funny
how our first bodily reaction
is the opposite
of what is actually best for us
of what is actually good for you
and what would be
much better
for all parties involved
including the blood
trying to flow
around your body
is to breathe
even more deeply
than usual

I wonder how many moments
we react like this
like warm bodies to frigid water
like known humans
to unfamiliar seas

Believe the story
that is most aligned
with reality

and if you must believe
a fictional story
make it worth the while because
belief defies reality
and if you wish to defy
reality
in this singular finite lifetime
it would be best
to make the story
unbelievably good.

– *inner dialogue*

uncertainty
is the heart
of mortality

in all of our many forms
wishes
and pursuits
we are at least
most certainly
one thing:

mortal
beings

- *pg.53*

Maybe
we should address
the unknown
more like
an old friend

(with embrace)

like the other languages we hear
but do not speak

(smile)

bridge the gap
and realise
the unknown
speaks most the same dialogue
just in ways
we haven't learnt yet
how

- the younger you start,
the easier it is

The more I learn about
what is considered normal
the less I believe
it is remotely ethical
or reasonable
to consider it
a valid reference
in what I personally consider
is right
or wrong

How easily
we forget realisations
and how readily
we remember
doubt

- practice and you will be good

To be smart enough
for our own good

that might just be
the key
to our human universe

Don't worry
you're on the right path
otherwise
you wouldn't notice
you were getting off track

remember
life is an adventure
and in all good adventures
somebody gets lost
and luckily
today
it's you!
and not somebody else
lost and amidst
what just might be
an incredible
adventure //

Not everything.
That's about the right amount

we've got to keep some impulsive
human qualities
otherwise
you and I
are more or less
computers
And heaven knows
we've got enough of those already

- pick and choose

I didn't understand
the depth in which
we affect others
until I was trying
to fall asleep
next to somebody
already sleeping
-

and as I changed and slowed
the depth of my breath
the dreamer
unconsciously
did the same
-

what a great interbeing
we share with others
to maintain our own
wellbeing
when something as subtle
as our breathing
affects each other
even in
totally
separate
states
of consciousness

Isn't it funny
how eagerly we sell
escapism
to ourselves
and each other

ideas that travelling to the far reaches
of the world
will provide answers
would provide contentment
could provide peace
to all the questions and desires and restlessness within -

Maybe it does
Maybe it will
but what I've learnt so far
from all my travels is this:
the best things in life aren't for sale
and in all my travels
I have not seen
one single advertisement
From the myriad of selling points
encouraging people
to take a trip
inwards

How many copies
do we make
before the art or importance
in taking care
of the original
becomes lost ?

- questions for self

Maybe
the truest of secrets
are truly impassable
and that is why
many a writer
philosopher
guru
and saviour
suffer deeply
trying
to share them
-

A true secret
will keep itself as such
even when
tryingly defined
in a matter
of words
-

And so forth,
as I realise this,
I will continue to write
sharing my reflections on living
knowing them
exactly as they are:

secrets

And discontinue
this impossibly tiring pursuit
of thinking
I could discover secrets
and then feel good
or responsible
for sharing them
-

If life chooses to entrust in me
the secrets of living well
I will do
as true friends do
and keep it exactly
as it was intended
to be
-

a secret

<u>We are</u>
<u>never here</u>
<u>again.</u>

that's the truth
of our situation

when you consider that
not as a belief
but as a reality

does anything
change?

Humans seem to be
the only form of life
that forms opinions
on whether or not
life is worth living
while simultaneously doing
just that.

Isn't it funny
how sitting down
to simply
close your eyes
to focus on your breath
and observe
the surrounding audioscape
is perceivably harder
than our usual mode of being
despite it being
a practice
of simply
doing less?

– buddhist hotline

To watch
our breath
is to focus
on the very ebb and flow
of life and living

we seem to watch
and watch out for
a lot of things
but find it peculiar explaining
why
to ourselves
or others
we might keep an eye
on something
of such
importance

Lick your own elbow
and tell me that
souls don't come
in pairs of two.

- two for one deals

Of all the steps
choose direction
of all the lovers
choose one
of all emotions
choose love

PART II.

Honeypot

I have a woman
like the sun
warm
beautiful
and giving of life
so much so
so intensely loving
that her affection
could burn through
all my layers
into my bloodstream
threatening both
my independence
and mortality
and
despite the consequences
just like the sun
since bathing
in your light
for the first time
I simply couldn't
live without you

living just isn't the same
without the sun

I could never understand
how
or why
it felt so real
when I was writing
about you
I thought I was just writing about ideals
about ideas
about fiction

now I chuckle
of course it felt real!
you were here all along
already chasing
laps around the sun
and I'm glad I didn't refrain
from writing
about you
just because yet
we had not met

romance in wonder and poetry and
loneliness
is alluring
and evergreen

but the embers that glow in the early hours
of the morning
are of trees
burnt not of youth
but of some age
and commitment

it will be so lovely
to spend the rest of this lifetime
writing
and knowing
and spending time with
the lady I am addressing
my love letters to.

If you wake up
and I'm not by your side
but instead
meditating
do not be alarmed

it's just that
sometimes
I wake up and I'm already running
already halfway though a conversation
already busy
and I've learnt
from the way that this feels
that it's no way
to greet the morning
that this is no way
to greet you
to be consumed in a busyness
that dims the colours of the bottlebrush
to be consumed in a fog
that numbs your pulse
against my fingers

I want space to hear the birds
and their battle cries
I want space to hear you moan
and grab you tighter

I want to make space
to respect the fact that
I can't take you or today
for granted

so don't worry
I'm coming back to bed
I'm just taking a moment
to start the day being still
to start the day being clear

To do what I know is right for me
So I can do right
by you

- yours truly, revised edition

Don't expect
in the midst of a storm
to make clear judgment
of the sea
her character
or yours
for you are only a drop of water
dancing the balance
of land and sea
you do not just belong to her
and she is only a body of water
dealing with the wind and a moon and a storm
she isn't entirely responsible for
she doesn't just belong to you
this is not to say
the storm isn't a true show of character
it certainly is
but remember
in the midst of a storm
you can drown in the sea
and blame her for it
despite the storm not being
something
of her making
the sea makes many things
but certainly not the storms
that you both have to
endure.

Let's make a pact
you and me
to never
ever
let complacency
sleep between
us

when we wake up
I want to make love
like the sun will travel
across a whole sky
like it isn't a given he will make it back
like we have to risk and endure
a sun rise
and a sun set
before making it back to each other
and when we do
I want to love
like the sun will travel
the other half of the world
like he could get lost
and even if
he makes it back
he has to convince the moon
and her many stars
to take him again
to trust him
to take the reigns

and wake the humans
from their slumber
and trance

and on the days we don't
or the days we can't

we can thank our lucky stars
that the sun is so dedicated
and put in the work
even when she couldn't see it
and that the moon
so beautiful and powerful and alluring
decided that
she needed him

how the sun and the moon
never let complacency
sleep between them
which gives us
the chance
to never
ever
let complacency
sleep between
us

We were facing
the head of the bed
you were sat between my legs
the outside of your thighs
slowly pressing against the inside of mine

your hands
were on my hips
guiding yourself
my thumbs were pressed into
your lower back

I was kissing your neck
and you were close
but keeping yourself
from coming again
you didn't want
to give that to me
so easily
until you were sure
I was holding you right
until I'd earned it
until I'd listened to
what you weren't saying
but needed me to hear

So I wrapped my left hand around your ribs
and pressed you to me tighter
bit your neck and asked you
please
you were starting to shake
as I traced my left hand down
between your legs
and my right hand up
and around
your neck
and then -

there was this beautiful moment
like standing out under a storm
when the clouds decide to pour from the heavens
and grace the earth with rain
that I felt the tension give
your head fell against my shoulder
your hair cascaded down my back
your weight fell against me
and you decided
to come
again

- rain

A woman doesn't have room in her bedroom
for you and your routine
for the boy
that resides
in me
in you
in every man
with a series of moves
that we perform in order
and in order
to keep ourselves comfortable
to keep us naively believing
we are mostly responsible
for whether or not
she comes

wipe that slate clean brother
take that boy into the next room
make sure he's got blankets and pillows
kiss him on the forehead
and wish him sweet dreams

because a woman has to deal with boys
all day
and tonight
she needs a man

A man who stands at the end of the bed
dresses himself down

and shows himself
bare and naked
and begins to attempt
to learn
and feel
and listen
to what she says
and what she doesn't

for when she holds her breath
for when she starts to shake
for when his tongue
between her legs
makes them squeeze
against his ears

for eye contact while being
deep inside of her
for a hand against her spine
and soft words
for feeling nervous
but remaining calm
in the most beautiful storm
when invited to navigate through
her endless
depths

I love your hair
wild and thick and untamed
a mind of its own
so much so
I can barely hold it all
even with my two hands
so much so
that it does a better job
of protecting your shoulders from the sun
than I ever will
so much so
that it barely dries after swimming
like it wants to take a little bit
of the sea with you
so much so
that I didn't realise
it keeps you slightly hidden
until you feel comfortable to unveil yourself

and today
across the table
you tied your hair up
for the first time
and it took my words away.

Sometimes
when I'm daydreaming
I imagine our home
wooden floors
an open living room
and a stool

a makeshift barber chair
drenched in sunlight
and every week or two
our living room turns into
a makeshift barber shop
and this act
is symbolic
of a truth

of how dangerous you are
in the best of ways

and when that blade
is pressed against my throat
much like
the intensity
of our love
you could
with ease and grace
bleed life from me

and I think
you are
the sweetest thing

because
even when
you have the chance
even when
I'm most vulnerable
you choose instead
not to pour a single drop for yourself

but instead
to save it
just for me
to keep on
loving
you

– high top sneakers

I wonder
if there is a word
that even comes close
to describing the feeling
of waking up
the barely conscious haze
after briefly falling asleep
left cheek
laid upon
your naked breasts
my arms wrapped around you
my hands against your ribs
and my stomach between your legs
where I can still feel you
pulsing
after both of us coming
at the same time.

I wonder if a word
will ever be able
to even attempt
describing that

Somewhere between
then and midnight
having sex
on the floor
just by
the balcony
you stood out on
naked and beautiful
you on top of me
me inside
of you
the breeze caressing
my hands on
your lower back

we stopped

and I sat on my knees
with my two hands
just above your hips
we closed our eyes
breathing
naked to each other
you placed your hands
on top of mine
and in that moment
I felt close to you

– *sex*

Remain dedicated
to the sea
even when you meet her
this will show her
your preparation

Remain dedicated
to the sea
as you are with her
this will show her
your commitment

Remain dedicated
to the sea
even when
she is gone

This will show her
true love
unlike many things
isn't something
remotely
temporary

PART III.

Concerned on behalf of The Universe

This morning
I was in the sea
floating on my back
and observed what a difference
one breath made;

Slowly breathing out
at a point
I was almost sinking

Then breathing in again
my whole body
began to float

One breath
made all the difference

Worry
isn't something
I often see
occurring naturally
outside of
human nature
-

Reflection
on the other hand
seems to be
a very common theme
-

in the mountains
in the sea

When we have
depression
or anxiety
we say
I have it
I have depression
I have anxiety
which makes sense
since we are so obsessed with having things

but
I wonder why
we must have these particular things
if this dialogue
allows movement
if this habit
allows healing

because these feelings
like many things we cling to
aren't ours to have
no wonder it hurts
trying to have these things
when they are only
passing
through

Nothing important I have done
in my life so far
helped me fit in

standing out is not important
but your important pursuits
will naturally do so

do not shy away
from what is important
to you
as you truly are

for standing out can be hard
but fitting in
is simply
impossible

- for my brother

Life is a race
but not the one
that is often
presented.
Life in full
from birth to death
is a marathon
and what we celebrate
is the short heroics
the incredible feats
right at the edge
of possible
and impossible.
This is not to suggest
that these sprints are not in fact incredible.
They certainly are
but it seems to me
we are the only lifeforms utterly obsessed
with racing to the finish line.
Which is truly bizarre
when you truly consider
how short our run actually is.
Not even the universe
infinite in existence and exempt of time
is in a rush to meet
its' end.

- joyride

Waves
that pass unridden
are not wasted
the only time
waves are wasted
are the ones that are
unappreciated
-

waves like life,
life like waves

Maybe
instead of being
worried
about how
to maintain peace of mind
in the future

I can just focus
on maintaining
peace of mind now

and in doing so
such peace
can naturally
reoccur

At some point
the flame jumps
from match or lighter
to the sage
and it is the sage
that becomes
alight

this
is the true nature
of inspiration

- *Embodiment*

There was not
any self-help books
any doctrine
any guru video poet passage
or piece of good advice
that could fill my cup
when what I needed
was space
of mind

no amount
of genuine input
can fill a space with peace
when turbulence
is the issue

if that be the case
fold this page
do some meditation
create some space

you can return to this later
x

You are
the only one
who can solve this.

And thank goodness
because otherwise
you'd be relying on others
for driving
instead of
directions.

Be present for
if anything
the memories
that will become
your past
to have something
to look back on

for how sad
it could be
to only have
memories of thoughts
and not thoughts
of memories

- it feels like a dream

There is no use pretending
that darkness doesn't exist.

The universe knows this
and that's why
even in the evening
when it could be pitch black
stars shine
from all over the galaxy
from millions of light years
away

what about the smog you say
where I live I can barely see the stars
well
the universe didn't get the memo re:
humans'- never-ending-disregard-for-pollution
what about the clouds you say
some nights it is truly dark
well,
true.
But even the clouds come and go

Ultimately
clouds are made of water
they are part of who we are
and without them
there wouldn't be rain
and we would be toast

so
anyways
my point is this:

the stars still shine
even when
you can't see them
the stars still shine
even when
it could just be dark

the stars still shine
the light is still there
even when your perception believes
otherwise

At some point in the depths
when you are freediving
you'll start having
contractions

and thank goodness, because
in the depths on a single breath
we need signals
amongst and amidst
our otherworldly endeavours
that remind us about
breathing

contractions
aren't signals that you're about to pass out
or that you should race to the surface
neither are true nor helpful
contractions
are just your body
reminding you to take note
of your humanly needs

consider this also
in your endeavours
above sea level
the signals are more subtle
and harder to read

I'm actually very certain
at 25 years old
there simply isn't
a meaning
of life

I thought there might have been
but now I think
how can there be

how on earth
could you boil down
the entire universe
to a definition

should we really presume that
one sentence
one phrase
or one whole fucking language
could casually define
existence?

Life didn't need
a meaning
a definition
a conclusion
or a place in a damn dictionary to exist

we do
we are the ones that seem so hell bent
on needing
a meaning

That motherfucker is sippin' pina coladas
while we are searching for answers
on something that exists
without question

Life was
life is
and life will continue to be
it isn't concerned
with needing
a meaning
to exist

So why
on earth
are we?

– Concerned on behalf of The Universe

Love
the art of accepting
the unknown

Peace
the art of not creating
new problems

Time
the art of embracing
elusiveness

Life
the little things amidst
the pursuit
of living

Fatigue
is a friend
that illuminates
the holes in our spirit

That now found
can be healed
with love
and light

Staring into the darkness
often gets a bad rep
I do it most days
when I'm meditating
staring at the back of my eyelids

– perspective

Truth
is a good friend
to everyone
-
and a good friend
is not defined
by your personal relationship
but the comradery
and light they bring
to everyone
along
the way

Our differences
are our currency
otherwise
we'd all be trading
back and forth
the same
coin

and of all the currency
in which we trade today
the one of truth and difference
seems to be
the least common
and the highest value

– stock market

Just breathe:
one of the most
challenging phrases
in the human language
to truly
practice

The Eagle
does not have the lifespan
to understand things
as the sea does
as the winds will
or as the cliffs do
but
The Eagle
has the wingspan
to harness the wind
to fly above
and observe it all

Grow your wings
and find the uplift
in where both worlds
collide

– *land & sea*

Today I've considered
to stop wishing for change in the past
to practice change in perspective
and started learning
Acceptance

Today I've considered
to cease categorising thoughts
as good or bad
and started learning
Choice

Today I considered
the entirety of unknown good and evil
then recognised myself
holding the pen
and started learning
Freedom

Today I realised
that space is filled entirely to the brim with light
and that it's only our hand
raised between
our eyes and the sun
that keeps us
from making room
for more

PART IV.

Lightwork

wake easy
rise slow.

Inspiration
cannot be postponed.
Remember that.

– *rain+checks*

Sitting backstage
before a sunset show
I suddenly saw life
and our experience like water
through a vessel

If you don't let
anything through
there is nothing to experience

If you don't let go
the vessel will not experience more

Let things in
let them go.
Perhaps,
this is the way.

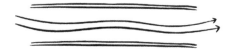

– lake wanaka dreams

In the carparks
opposite surf spots
we still practice
our momentary rebellion
against the shackles of society
skating the concrete
lost in the waves

Clear your mind
then do the dishes

Better a clear mind
than a clean house
since it's only one of them
we truly tend
to live in

- Home

And on that day
we hung around home
and drank a lot of coffee
and on that day
the ordinary
was simply
divine

- the little things

The older I get
the more I see
that trying
is neither useful
or productive.

try less
do more

…. and as the sun rose from the east,
I saw light flicker over the sea
and the way it played
on the horizon to the shoreline
made me think
from head to toe
perhaps we could play
in the light
as well.

Thank you
for today
for the challenges
and the easy things
and my chance to enjoy them all
to extend the human spirit
into light

thank you for the health of my loved ones
the meaningfulness of their pursuits
and their ability to see themselves
just as they are

thank you for
the food water air and shelter
that comes from the earth
and thank you for
your natural states
your natural places
your natural sounds
that help me
return
to mine

– my non-religious prayer

In the light
of the moon
or the sun
almost everything
casts a shadow

and almost
everything
that casts a shadow
can only do so
due to
its depth

To love what we have in abundance
this must be
one of the greatest challenges
of the human spirit
I wonder what would change
in the world and each other
in imagination
in health
in time
in freedom
in all these resources
beyond definitive value
if we just
simply
loved
what was readily available
as much as we love
what is scarce
or simply
no longer

– value

Spend time
amongst the timeless
and notice
how the cliffs
close to the sea
absorb her sounds
and sing them
back to her
-
humans
can do
the same

Spinifex bends in the wind
sand forms shapes
in the same way
crabs make homes
footprints lead to their house
footprints cover the beach
along with paw prints of everyone
who's been here
today
yesterday
and forever
-
are they all just here
for stories
to tell?

- spinifex beach haiku

Let us curate art
but not moments
pose for pictures
but not memories
perform on stage
but never
in acts
of kindness

to attempt
to capture
the soul of things
is just fine
but to trade
genuine experience
in that pursuit
I dare to say
could be
a mistake

Yesterday
I observed the patterns of fallen rain
of water in the sand
making its way to the sea
-

and the water channelled
in different little streams
before meeting at a point
and becoming
One
-

and
these little patterns
these little channels
were shaped like
the roots of a tree
-

and it's these roots
that give a tree
its life
-

and it made me wonder
if life is truly reaching for the heavens
or if life is even more so
reaching
inward

- grounding

Today we walked
in water
not even
ankle deep
and as we walked
our footsteps rippled
growing until
they became four or so waves
pushing across the sand
stretching in size and length
perpendicular to the tide
before meeting the incoming waves
subtly continuing sideways
and out of sight
-

if bare feet
can change an ocean
it would be entirely reasonable
to give thought and consideration
in how and where
and with what care
we take
each
step.

The glass
is not half empty
or half full
it's overflowing

the same way
it's overflowing and submerged
when the sink is filled with water
and you are washing the dishes

the only difference is
you are the glass
and in what you are immersed
is not just water
within a sink

-

drink
up

The *truly* important things
you do not need to write down
in order to
remember.

Many people
can cut down the trees
tall and touching the heavens
but very few
can nurture
the seedling
and cultivate
the patience
it takes
to grow something
so beautiful
and giving
of life
-
Watch the people
eager to boast
of such feats
for once you begin
to grow something
from the ground up
cutting them down
doesn't seem to be
such
a show
of strength

- tall poppy syndrome

When you set out
in pursuit of your dreams
know you become responsible
not just for the dreams of yourself
but also
for the dreams
of others

because we all have dreams
and some people
never set foot
in their direction

and so you adopt
the responsibility
of the dreamer

and by pursuing yours
you light a torch
and remember this
when you feel a heavy burden
of course it's heavy
when society
is not centred
around pursuing
our dreams

but someone may stop
and see your light
feel the warmth
and take to the kindle

suddenly,
flammable

and your role in this my friend
is of utmost importance
because people
are rarely encouraged
in any way shape or form
to pursue a life
worth dreaming for

yet it is
the pursuit of our dreams
and the previously unimagined
that keeps both hope
and the human spirit
Alight.

- fremantle

Light travels
across a solar system
clouds draw water
from the earth
into the sky
to rain back down

and as sun poured
onto flowers next to me
I thought of
all the distance
that's been travelled
and how
that alone
must be
enough reason
to just enjoy
watching these flowers
being bathed
in sunlight

– *toronto*

ACKNOWLEDGEMENTS

Thank you to my team, who brought this book to life amongst the relative chaos of touring the world — it was almost lost in the years between, and I can breathe a sigh of relief now these sun memos are bundled into these pages.

Writing poetry has nothing to do with publishing it. Writing poetry is what music has been for me since the very beginning: an outpour.

Minimal planning, maximum emotion.

Like my first book, *brainwaves*, this is another thoughtfully independent project made possible by my family & friends at Commonfolk Publishing.

Looking forward to connecting with you all for the second time, and again.

X,
zig

ABOUT THE AUTHOR

world touring musician
(still) human being
ocean enthusiast
author

Ziggy Alberts, an Australian singer-songwriter and author, has captivated audiences worldwide with his authentic writing, folk-pop melodies and an upbeat energy that shines in his solo-act, live performances.

Alberts' narrative unfolds on his terms, reflected in his latest musical records and debut poetry release, *brainwaves*. Differentiating from his lyrical work, readers of *brainwaves*, and now through *sun memos*, can discover some of Alberts' most personal realisations from life at home and on the road within his prose.

Ziggy Alberts continues to earn critical acclaim with 'Laps Around the Sun' proudly ARIA Double Platinum Certified, while 'Gone', 'Runaway', 'Heaven', 'Stronger', 'Love Me Now', 'Simple Things', 'Days In The Sun' and EP 'Four Feet in the Forest' have achieved ARIA Platinum Certification. He has also received Gold Certifications for his 'Laps Around The Sun' album and a further six tracks in his catalogue. Alberts has also received an APRA Music Award for Most Performed Blues & Roots Work for his track 'Letting Go'.

Printed in the USA
CPSIA information can be obtained
at www.ICGtesting.com
CBHW050926150524
8554CB00005B/5